THE
PASSION
of JESUS

KENNETH SCHENCK

wesleyan
publishing
house

Indianapolis, Indiana

Copyright © 2013 by Kenneth Schenck
Published by Wesleyan Publishing House
Indianapolis, Indiana 46250
Printed in the United States of America
ISBN: 978-0-89827-737-1
ISBN (e-book): 978-0-89827-814-9

Library of Congress Cataloging-in-Publication Data

Schenck, Kenneth, 1966-
  The passion of Jesus / Kenneth Schenck.
    pages cm
  ISBN 978-0-89827-737-1
1. Jesus Christ--Passion. 2. Devotional literature. I. Title.
  BT431.3.S34 2013
  232.96--dc23
                              2013033136

CONTENTS

INTRODUCTION

The two most important events in the entire history of the world took place within the span of three days: Jesus' death and Jesus' resurrection. Jesus' death broke the power of sin and death, the two arch nemeses of the human race. Then Jesus' resurrection reflects the victory over sin and death that God has made possible so that we can rise to new life in this world and to eternal life after Christ returns a second time.

One person has called the gospel of Mark a passion narrative with a long introduction. The final week of Jesus' ministry takes up about a third of the entire book. This fact shows us how central Jesus' death and resurrection are to the gospel. In 1 Corinthians 15:3–7, these are exactly the events that Paul described as the basic content of the gospel. The good news is that the risen Jesus has been enthroned as cosmic king, after dying for our sins.

Some scholars have even speculated that Mark's passion story might have been the very first part of the gospel to be written, perhaps even years before Mark or any other gospel reached its current form. Mark 11–16 first records Jesus' entrance to Jerusalem on Palm Sunday, a week before his resurrection. Then on Monday he "cleansed" the temple, overturning the tables of the money changers and driving them and the animals off the temple grounds.

On Tuesday, Jesus debated with various Jewish groups like the Pharisees, priests, and Sadducees. He also predicted that the temple would be destroyed and gave a number of signs to look out for. That evening he dined at a leper's house, and a woman anointed his head, which he said was symbolic of his coming burial.

Thursday night he ate a Last Supper with his disciples before praying in the garden of Gethsemane. But Judas Iscariot had betrayed him, and soldiers came to arrest him in the garden. Jesus appeared before the Jewish leaders and Pilate, and finally he was crucified on Friday morning. But Sunday morning the women found his tomb empty, and a young man announced that the disciples would see him in Galilee.

This book presents six weeks of Bible studies on Mark's passion and resurrection story. Each week will follow a part of the passion story. Within each week, there are five days of reflection on the text, looking at only a few verses each day. The aim is to experience life transformation by hearing God speak to us through the words he revealed through Mark to a group of (probably) Gentile believers in the second half of the first century. Hear God speak to you through Scripture and then live faithfully to his Word through the power of the Holy Spirit.

Week 1

ENTERING JERUSALEM
Mark 11:1–25

Those who went ahead and those who followed shouted,
"Hosanna! Blessed is he who comes in the name of
the Lord! Blessed is the coming kingdom of our father
David! Hosanna in the highest heaven!"

—MARK 11:9–10

Day 1

THE LORD HAS NEED
Mark 11:1–6

INTRODUCTION

Jesus went to Jerusalem for the final week of his earthly mission. In these verses, he sent two of his followers to get a colt from a nearby village.

ENGAGE

Jesus had a plan to enter the city of Jerusalem in a certain way, and that plan involved a colt to fulfill prophecy. He did not go get it himself. Perhaps he was being careful about his entrance. Perhaps he did not want to eclipse the big moment on Palm Sunday, which could easily happen if he was mobbed getting the animal. The colt's keepers, whether they knew of the plan ahead of time or not, submitted to the need of their Lord. They let Jesus be the first to sit on their young colt. They had something the Lord wanted to use, and they were willing to give it to him.

Take my life, and let it be consecrated,
Lord, to thee. . . . Take my will, and make
it thine; it shall be no longer mine.

—FRANCES HAVERGAL

EXAMINE

Mark did not tell us whether Jesus had prearranged to get the colt or not. In one possible scenario, Jesus had already made arrangements to get the animal. In this interpretation, the statement, "The Lord needs it" (11:3), clued in the colt's owners that they were giving it to the right person. It would be part of an earlier agreement. In another scenario, Jesus prophetically knew that the colt would be there. The colt's owners would give it to the disciples in spontaneous submission to Jesus' authority. We simply don't have enough information in Mark to know which interpretation he wanted us to make. Either one seems possible given what Mark said.

EXPLORE

The Lord occasionally wants to borrow a "colt" from us to accomplish his mission. It is of course *his*, since everything we have ultimately belongs to God. Sometimes the colt is a small thing. Perhaps God would like us to give a few cents to the person in line in front of us who is short some tiny amount. Sometimes the Lord needs to borrow our life as a martyr or as a missionary or to show others what it means to suffer with cancer and keep faith. Having a Lord means being completely surrendered to his purposes and plan. It means that when the Lord has need of something in our power, we immediately give it.

PRAYER

Lord, I give you my colt to use in whatever way you see fit. I am your willing servant.

Day 2

HOSANNA!
Mark 1:7–11

INTRODUCTION

These verses are about what Christians have come to call "Palm Sunday." The Sunday before Easter every year, Christians remember Jesus' triumphal entry into Jerusalem the week of his crucifixion.

ENGAGE

Jesus entered Jerusalem like a king. The branches the people laid down acted out Psalm 118:27: "With boughs in hand, join in the festal procession." Their words quoted the previous verse: "Blessed is he who comes in the name of the LORD" (118:26). Although Mark did not quote Zechariah 9:9, Matthew did, and it seems likely that Jesus intentionally entered Jerusalem in the way he did in order to "act out" the fulfillment of this verse as a prophecy. This fact is significant, because it means Jesus was implicitly claiming to be the Messiah, the expected king of Israel. There was a drama of coronation going on here, and Jesus was following God's intended script.

EXAMINE

Was Jesus reflecting on Psalm 118 as he neared Jerusalem? There are other familiar verses in the psalm beyond those the crowds quoted. For example, 118:22 says, "The stone the builders rejected has become the cornerstone." The psalm speaks of strong opposition and enemies, as well as vindication by God. It pictures near defeat and yet salvation from God. It speaks of potential death and yet God's rescue. Gates are opened, and the king makes his way to the temple. This is exactly the path that Jesus took in Mark. It is interesting to speculate whether we are looking into the thoughts of Jesus as he entered Jerusalem that day, acting out words probably associated with King David of old.

EXPLORE

The crowds and disciples probably did not see what was coming. Surely none of them would have guessed that glorious Palm Sunday that Jesus would die later in the week, let alone rise again the next Sunday! It may have been easy for the crowds to participate in Jesus' triumphal entry because they didn't know the cost. They didn't know that death would come before life. They didn't know that defeat would come before victory. Perhaps they expected the heavens to break open and for angelic armies to descend on Jerusalem. Are we prepared to follow through with God's plan even if it leads through rough waters before the safe harbor? Or are we only with Christ when the going looks easy?

Jesus also suffered outside the city gate to make the people holy through his own blood. Let us, then, go to him outside the camp, bearing the disgrace he bore.

—HEBREWS 13:12–13

PRAYER

Jesus, I commit to go with you in festal procession beyond the triumphant gates to your triumphant suffering outside the gates, laying down my life as a palm branch.

Day 3

RELIGIOUS THIEVERY
Mark 11:15–19

INTRODUCTION

Jesus drove money changers and those selling sacrificial animals out of the temple courts, solidifying opposition to him among the religious leaders of Jerusalem.

ENGAGE

More than any other, this event likely set in motion Jesus' arrest and crucifixion later in the week. In Mark, Jesus threw the money changers and sellers of animals out of the temple courts on Monday. These practices were necessary for the temple's operations, since travelers from far away would scarcely bring sacrificial animals with them, and they would need to change money in order to purchase them. The temple leaders were sensitive to disruptions like the one Jesus made, not least because they knew how the Romans felt about public disturbances. Even beyond any disagreement they might have with Jesus' teaching, this sort of action would have immediately marked him as dangerous and someone to be watched carefully.

In your anger, do not sin. Do not let the sun
go down while you are still angry,
and do not give the devil a foothold.

—EPHESIANS 4:26–27

EXAMINE

The Scriptures Jesus quoted in Mark give us some hints of what so angered Jesus about the situation at the temple. Mark mentioned two Scriptures. The first was Isaiah 56:7, whose context speaks of how Israel should welcome any foreigner who wishes to worship at the temple, as well as the scattered exiles of Israel. The second was Jeremiah 7:11, whose context has to do with those who hide behind the temple while oppressing the immigrant, the widow, and the orphan. A reasonable guess is to think that these individuals in Mark were taking advantage of travelers from afar, perhaps charging far more than they should. Others have suggested that Jesus was acting out the destruction of the temple that would later take place.

EXPLORE

This event in the temple is the one incident where we know Jesus really got angry. He showed us that anger in itself is not sinful. It's what we do when we are angry. It is also significant to notice what made him angry. It was not sin in general. It was not because someone was breaking a law or a rule. It was not because someone disobeyed the Bible. It was the fact that someone was being oppressed. More than anything, Jesus became angry when those with power took advantage of those who were powerless. What makes us angry? Is it when we do not get our way? Is it because someone breaks the rules? Is it because someone is hurting someone else?

PRAYER

Father, help me be angry at the right things. Don't let me get away with pretending to be angry at unrighteousness when I am really hiding selfishness and hypocrisy.

Day 4

THE FIG TREE
Mark 11:12–14, 20–21

INTRODUCTION

Jesus' cursing of the fig tree and its withering was probably an illustration of what would happen to Israel because of its failure to bear the appropriate fruit of righteousness.

ENGAGE

It might seem a little harsh, maybe even selfish for Jesus to curse a fig tree simply because it did not have any fruit on it and he was hungry. But as we will see in the next section, there is probably more to this story than meets the eye. Nevertheless, God intends for his people to bear fruit. The fruit in question is fruit of righteousness. We might even think of the fruit of the

Spirit in Galatians 5:22–23. God's trees bear the right kind of fruit. God tears down trees that bear the wrong kind of fruit. The wrong kind of fruit, as we see in the next section, is fruit that hurts others and does not love neighbors.

EXAMINE

One literary device Mark used occasionally might be called "sandwiching." He would start to tell one story then put a different story in the middle before returning to the first story. In the process, both stories illustrate one another. In this case, Jesus' cursing of the fig tree sandwiches Jesus' "cleansing" of the temple courts. Surely we are meant to think that just as the fig tree did not bear fruit, in some way, what was going on at the temple was also a failure to bear fruit. Accordingly, just as Jesus cursed the fig tree and it withered, so Jesus' action in the temple was surely taken at some point to imply God's judgment on Israel, which happened in A.D. 70.

EXPLORE

Bearing fruit in this context is not about numbers. For example, it's not about how many people you convert to Christ. It's not about how much your church is growing. Bearing fruit in this passage is about living a righteous life. It's about loving your neighbor. We live in a world that isn't looking for that sort of result. It's looking for profit and output. The absence of fruit in this story was oppression of the outsider. The religious leadership was standing between God and those who wanted to worship him. Are we obstacles to someone else's faith? Are we stumbling blocks that will potentially trip others in their pursuit of God? Do our lives make God more or less attractive?

But the fruit of the Spirit is love, joy, peace, forbearance, kindness, goodness, faithfulness, gentleness and self-control. Against such things there is no law.

—GALATIANS 5:22–23

PRAYER

Spirit, give me eyes to see what good fruit looks like. Then water and feed my life; bend my will so that I yield it to you.

Day 5

MOUNTAIN-MOVING FAITH
Mark 11:22–25

INTRODUCTION

The disciples were amazed that Jesus' words could cause a fig tree to wither. Their surprise gave Jesus an opportunity to talk about the power of faith and what God wants to do through anyone who has enough faith.

ENGAGE

Jesus gave the startling teaching that faith can move mountains. Just as he cursed a trivial fig tree and it withered, the disciples could do incredible things if they had enough faith. If you believe when you are praying, the answer will come. Of course this is not always the case, and we should assume that Jesus did not mean this teaching to apply to every prayer in every situation. God will not grant evil requests or prayers made with an unloving heart. The key is that our hearts align with God's heart when we pray. When God's heart and ours are in sync, then the things we are praying for are things he wants to give.

EXAMINE

Mark 11:25 gives us teaching on the need to forgive others if we expect God to forgive us. Matthew possibly moved this teaching to the Sermon on the Mount (Matt. 6:14–15), where it goes along well with the Lord's Prayer. You might notice that almost all versions except the King James Version do not have Mark 11:26, because it is missing from significant early copies of Mark. The parable of the unforgiving servant in Matthew 18:21–35 makes the point emphatically. God will not forgive our wrongdoing unless we are willing to forgive the wrongs others have done to us. The lesson is that we can create obstacles to our prayers by hardening our hearts.

EXPLORE

There are levels of faith, and there is such a thing as the gift of faith. All Christians must have a certain amount of faith in God and Christ in order to become part of his people—Jesus has to be our Lord. But even among those who have this basic faith, there are some who have a gift of faith that goes beyond the rest of us. These are the John "Praying" Hydes and the George Müllers of the world whom God seems to bless with a certainty that God wants to do the seemingly impossible—and does it. The great news is that the Bible encourages us to ask God to increase our faith (Luke 17:5). He wants to increase it!

Prayer is not overcoming God's reluctance,
but laying hold of his willingness.

—MARTIN LUTHER

PRAYER

Lord, as the disciples asked you long ago, I ask you to increase my faith. Help me to see the possible where others see the impossible.

BRIDGING JESUS' WORLD AND OURS

In the passages for this week, we have especially seen some of Jesus' emotions, his anger in particular. He became angry with a fig tree that had not borne fruit and with a temple that had failed God's people. The old saying "What would Jesus do?" remains a good one, and we get some good hints here.

More than anything else, Jesus became upset when those in power abused or did not help those who were the weakest. He became angry when people put up artificial barriers between each other, especially when those barriers favored some and disadvantaged others. His anger with the fig tree should not be interpreted as anger for not producing results in some capitalistic or church-growth sense. It was an anger that the leadership of Israel had not produced good works, works of righteousness that break down walls and help those in need.

Jesus' example provides us with a model for our values. But as we have said, Jesus also showed us that anger is not evil in itself. Evil is a matter of our intentions, and it is what we do with our anger that may lead to sin.

EXERCISE

Take an inventory of your emotions this week. In particular, what kinds of things make you angry? Do you become angry when others are treated unfairly? Or do you become angry because things don't go your way or are inconvenient to you? Resolve to change with God's help, if necessary.

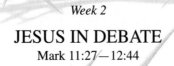

Week 2

JESUS IN DEBATE
Mark 11:27—12:44

The stone the builders rejected has become
the cornerstone; the Lord has done this,
and it is marvelous in our eyes.

—MARK 12:10–11

Day 1

JESUS' AUTHORITY
Mark 11:27—12:12

INTRODUCTION

After his action in the temple, Jerusalem leaders asked Jesus what the basis of his authority was. He did not tell them, but gave a parable about some tenants who rejected the landowner. In response, the owner replaced them.

ENGAGE

One of the ways in which Jesus deflected questions was by asking questions back that his interrogators either could not answer or did not want to answer. When the leaders asked Jesus the basis for his authority, he asked them whether they thought that John the Baptist had the authority of heaven. They didn't want to say yes, because that would suggest they had disobeyed heaven. They didn't want to say no, because that might anger the crowds. But they surely got the point: Jesus' message and actions had the same prophetic authority from heaven that John the Baptist had. And no doubt they were just as eager for Jesus to be taken out of the picture as they were with John the Baptist.

Search me, O God and know my heart today.
Try me, O Savior, know my thoughts, I pray.
See if there be some wicked way in me.
Cleanse me from every sin and set me free.

—JAMES ORR

EXAMINE

The parable of the tenants is an interpretation of the response of the leadership of Jerusalem to Jesus. God is the owner and planter of the vineyard. The farmers were the leaders of Jerusalem, those mentioned at the end of Mark 11: chief priests, teachers of the law, and Jerusalem elders. (The sense that they were only renters of the land in the parable is striking!) Like the tenants, they rejected God's messengers, prophets like John the Baptist and also the son, Jesus. In Mark's gospel, this parable was a fore-shadowing of what was about to happen to Jesus, and it showed that Jesus knew what they were planning (compare 11:18). It also foreshadowed what would happen to the leaders of Jerusalem soon enough (12:9).

EXPLORE

How do you react when you are found out? Often, the first reaction is denial and anger. Have you seen it happen? A person is confronted about an affair or financial impropriety. Perhaps even most of the time, the initial reaction is to harden and attack in response. The Jerusalem leaders are a warning of what *not* to do. Jesus read their intentions in Mark. He exposed the true role they were playing in the story, but they did not repent. They didn't even examine themselves to see if Jesus could be right. They continued on the same path. We should always be open to correction, because if we are in the wrong, we will want to change.

PRAYER

Father, I submit myself to true righteousness. I want to be a good tenant of your land. Show me the path, and I will walk on it.

Day 2

PAYING TAXES
Mark 12:13–17

INTRODUCTION

After the chief priests and elders had taken a stab at Jesus, the Pharisees went next. They tried to snare Jesus on the issue of taxes.

ENGAGE

The Pharisees in this story were trying to paint Jesus either as a revolutionary or as someone the crowds shouldn't think of as a potential king. Someone who thinks he is the Messiah, they surely thought, would not accept paying taxes to another king, to a foreign power. But if Jesus admitted that he was the true king, then they could have the Romans arrest him as a seditious revolutionary. Jesus' answer was dismissive of their categories. He rejected coinage itself as something completely foreign to the kingdom of God. His kingdom is of a completely different order and economy altogether, where the poor are blessed (Luke 6:20) and the rich are sent away empty (Luke 1:53).

Earn all you can; save all you can;
give all you can.

—JOHN WESLEY

EXAMINE

The world in which Jesus lived was a farming, fishing, and trading world. It was not a world where the exchange of money was the primary mode of living. When Jesus asked whose picture was on the coin, he was pointing out that the system of coinage and money was foreign to Israel and God's kingdom. Sure, he could pay taxes if he happened to come across a coin. If I find something of value to you but not to me, wouldn't I pass it on to you? Let's say you collect stamps and I get a letter from someone overseas with a very interesting one. Might I not pass it along? Jesus treated Caesar's coins similarly.

EXPLORE

It is interesting to hear people say occasionally that it is against their Christian conscience to pay taxes or that it is stealing for the government to use their money for something that does not benefit them personally. These positions have no biblical support whatsoever. The New Testament (including Jesus and Paul) consistently says to pay taxes. It does so in part because Jesus saw money—as well as worldly powers, like the empire—as something that was completely different from God's kingdom. And Jesus gave these instructions in a world where taxes were used in a far more unjust way than today. Christians will take different positions on the specifics of taxes today, but we should agree that all we have belongs to God.

PRAYER

Father, loosen my grip on earthly things that I mistakenly think are mine. Help me to see that everything belongs to you and that my possessions are really yours.

Day 3

RESURRECTION?
Mark 12:18–27

INTRODUCTION

The Pharisees and temple leaders had taken their shots at Jesus. Now it was the Sadducees' turn. They debated with Jesus on the topic of resurrection.

ENGAGE

The law of Levite marriage in Deuteronomy 25 specified that if an older brother died without an heir, a younger brother needed to take his brother's wife as his own in order to produce an heir. The story the Sadducees made up involves this dynamic. They also mixed in another well-known Jewish story about seven brothers who died a martyr's death in hope of resurrection. The Sadducees thought that resurrection didn't make sense because of issues like whose wife a woman with many husbands would be in the resurrection. Once again, Jesus undermined the categories of his opponents. In the resurrection, women won't be subordinate to men in marriage, as they were in the ancient world. Like the angels, we won't have marriage partners anymore.

We will not all sleep, but we will all be changed—in a flash, in the twinkling of an eye, at the last trumpet. For the trumpet will sound, the dead will be raised imperishable, and we will be changed.

—1 CORINTHIANS 15:51–52

EXAMINE

From what scholars can tell, the Sadducees were an upper-class group of priestly families who had significant power in the temple. High priests were often Sadducees. They did not follow the "traditions of the elders" of the Pharisees, believing that the Pharisees had gone well beyond what the law itself taught. From this perspective, their most distinctive aspect was the fact that they did not believe in any kind of resurrection or meaningful life after death. They did not believe that the spirits of people continued to exist or that anyone became an angel after death. They did not believe that corpses would come back to life at some point in the future or that anyone would eventually receive a transformed body.

EXPLORE

I have heard a strange rumor among Christians, based, I think, on this passage. I've met Christians who think that we won't remember each other in heaven, that husbands and wives won't recognize each other in the afterlife. Suffice it to say, the Bible doesn't teach this idea anywhere. This passage only says that there isn't any marriage in the kingdom, not that husbands and wives won't know each other anymore. There just won't be any sexual relations and, in particular, women will not be subjugated to men anymore. Given what Jesus said elsewhere in the Gospels (for example, Matt. 8:11), he probably did not picture the resurrection being in heaven, but on a renewed earth.

PRAYER

God of the living, raise me up to new life, not only in the next life, but in the way I think and act in this one.

Day 4

THE LOVE COMMANDMENT
Mark 12:28–34

INTRODUCTION

The last question the Jerusalem leaders asked Jesus was what he thought was the most important commandment of all. Jesus' answer was the love commandments—to love God and to love neighbor.

ENGAGE

Jesus and Paul both said that that the love command was the fulfillment of the Old Testament law, especially the part about loving one's neighbor. Loving one's neighbor is doing to them what you would have them do to you. It is wanting the best for them rather than wishing them harm. It is always choosing what is best for them when you have a choice. It is not being selfish or stingy with what you have. It can be disciplining someone who needs to learn something, and it can involve justice to protect others from harm. Even when you think you are following it literally, Jesus allowed no application of Scripure if it involves hatred toward others. Jesus trumps your interpretation.

EXAMINE

Some who call themselves Christians hide behind the idea of loving God in order to do things unloving to their neighbors. These are the Pharisees who dedicated to God the support they would normally have given to their parents, and then couldn't support their parents. But truly loving God will never contradict loving your neighbor. God's expectations are such that living them out is never unloving to others. We may have to make hard choices. For example, we may have to discipline or even exact justice for the sake of others. But we will never do so out of hatred or vengeance. No one can genuinely love God while behaving in a hateful way toward others.

EXPLORE

We shouldn't think of the "parts" of a human being here as anything like an absolute or even literal list. We are to love God with our whole hearts, souls, minds, and strength. The basic point is that we are to love God with our entire being. Our strength reminds us that we are to serve God with our bodies and what we do with them. We must love God with our actions. God still wants us to serve him with our intellect and with our thinking. Back then, *mind* probably included attitudes as well. Most important is that we love God with our hearts, meaning our wills and our intentions. If this part of us serves God, then every other part will follow.

If you love only those who love you, what reward do you have? . . . If you greet only your brothers and sisters, what more are you doing? Don't even the Gentiles do the same? Therefore, just as your heavenly Father is complete in showing love to everyone, so also you must be complete.

—MATTHEW 5:46–48 CEB

PRAYER

Jesus, I want to love as you loved. Spirit, empower me to love in the spaces between where I already love, and remove all hatred from my heart.

Day 5

JESUS' PRIORITIES
Mark 12:35–44

INTRODUCTION

After all of Jesus' debate partners had a shot, it was Jesus' turn to ask the questions. He asked them one that none of them could answer. Then he criticized their pretenses to godliness, instead praising a widow who gave to God the little she had.

ENGAGE

At the end of these three paragraphs, Jesus praised a widow for having the right attitude. In comparison to many others, she gave very little — just two small coins. But she gave just about everything she had, even digging into the money she lived on. She was the one Jesus commended. God is no doubt happy with the fact that the wealthy give, but they are hardly worthy of great honor when their giving is at no sacrifice to them, even if they give what seems to the rest of us like large amounts. God certainly doesn't commend those trying to impress others with their smarts or religiosity. God commended this widow who no one might even have noticed if Jesus hadn't pointed her out.

EXAMINE

The challenges of Jesus' opponents in Mark 12 had come from almost every major Jewish group. They asked him about doctrine, ethics, and leadership. He bested them every time. Now it was his turn: Who was David talking about in Psalm 110:1? Maybe they had been grumbling that Jesus couldn't be the Messiah because he wasn't a descendent of David (not knowing that he actually was). Maybe he just wanted them to know they didn't know as much as they thought they did. But they had no answer for his question and were left silenced. No doubt most of us could use some silencing from time to time, especially when we think we have all the answers.

EXPLORE

Mark gives us a hint of Jesus' teaching about hypocrisy, which Matthew 6 gives us more fully. The teachers of the law in Jerusalem were apparently more interested in being admired by other people than by God. They dressed nicely.

They took the best seats on public occasions. Meanwhile, they in effect robbed the homes of the weak and defenseless. How easy it is for us to follow this pattern of hypocrisy today, even with such clear examples before us. Jesus hinted that we are not as likely to see godliness when we go to the "shiny objects" that our eyes are drawn to, but with what is going on in the less-noticeable, often-despised places.

PRAYER

Father, in the moment I am most tempted to think I have arrived spiritually, remind me of the widow who put those two copper coins in the treasury.

BRIDGING JESUS' WORLD AND OURS

In the passages for this week, we have especially seen Jesus using his mind, his ability to debate in particular. He sparred intellectually with almost every major Jewish group of the time, including chief priests, Pharisees, and Sadducees. His authority was in question. How could this obscure man from the backwater north exhibit such authority?

But Jesus did not merely claim authority with his words. Indeed, for the most part, he made few claims of that sort. What he did was to demonstrate his authority both in his words and deeds. In the debates he had on that day, he bested the brightest of Israel. He did not best them because he was out to win, but because he truly did have the answers to the most pressing questions of the day.

Jesus retains that authority today. Some of the details of the issues have changed (although we still have taxes). The faces have changed. But there are still those who miss Jesus' command to love because they are too focused on rules. There are still those who are more interested in their ideas than in helping people. But the central values—love God and love neighbor—remain fully the same.

It is in giving that we receive. . . . It is in dying [to ourselves] that we are born to eternal life.

—St. Francis of Assisi

EXERCISE

Take an inventory of your mind this week. In particular, what are your thoughts and attitudes? Do you live a life of total love (implying submission) for God? Do you act contrary to the love of your neighbor (including your enemies)? Resolve to change with God's help, if necessary.

Week 3

JESUS AND THE TEMPLE
Mark 13:1–37

Keep watch because you do not know when the owner of the house will come back—whether in the evening, or at midnight, or when the rooster crows, or at dawn. If he comes suddenly, do not let him find you sleeping.

—MARK 13:35–36

Day 1

DOOMED TO DESTRUCTION
Mark 13:1–4

INTRODUCTION

On leaving the temple, one of the disciples admired its massive stones and buildings. Then Jesus predicted its destruction, and they asked him what signs would anticipate the event.

ENGAGE

These verses are important because they make it clear that Mark 13 is not talking about some temple that will be built in the end times. The temple that the disciples asked about was the one standing right in front of them. It was its destruction that they asked Jesus about, when it would happen and what signs would indicate it was about to take place. The context of Mark 13 thus leads us to expect that the signs and events that follow all relate to the time just before A.D. 70. At the same time, it is at least possible that past and present are blurred in the predictions, as we will see in other devotions this week.

EXAMINE

The Romans destroyed the Jerusalem temple in the summer of A.D. 70, and the prediction of Mark 13 came true. Today, the Wailing Wall is all that is visible of the structures of the previous temple mount, although it was not part of the temple itself. Jews now regularly pray there. The temple of Jesus' day was itself a replacement for Solomon's temple, which the Babylonians destroyed in 586 B.C. So, predictions in the Old Testament about the temple being rebuilt were fulfilled centuries before Jesus, in 516 B.C. The Muslim Dome of the Rock and Al-Aqsa Mosque have occupied the temple mount now for over a thousand years, and orthodox Jews do not believe anyone should step foot on it.

EXPLORE

A lot of modern prophecy suggests that the Antichrist will rebuild the Jerusalem temple and set himself up in it as God (compare 2 Thess. 2:4). The problem is that while the Gospels mention the destruction of the temple, they nowhere mention anything about it being rebuilt.

In fact, the New Testament books of Hebrews and Revelation imply that there is no place for a temple in the age of Christ. Yet prophecies don't always come true in exactly the way the Old Testament prophets might have thought. Even Jesus applied a prophecy differently than Daniel might have anticipated. It's best not to speculate too much about the future, since we'll only know for sure after it all comes to pass.

In his time, in his time, he makes all things beautiful, in his time. Lord, please show me every day, as you're teaching me your way that you do just what you say in your time.

—DIANE BALL

PRAYER

Lord, help me resist the urge to know things you have not yet shared with me, and give me humility to realize that I do not even know as much as I think I do.

Day 2

RUMORS OF WARS
Mark 13:5–13

INTRODUCTION

In these verses, Jesus laid out the kinds of events that would lead up to the destruction of the temple in A.D. 70. There would be false messiahs and persecution. Faith in Jesus would even divide families.

ENGAGE

Peter, James, and John had asked Jesus what signs would take place leading up to the destruction of the temple. Jesus painted a picture of great crisis and turmoil. The disciples would be flogged in the synagogues, as we know the apostle Paul was on several occasions. They would be arrested and put on trial. Acts 12 tells us that indeed James was beheaded by Herod Agrippa I. Tradition has it that Peter died at the hands of the emperor Nero in the A.D. 60s. Although the idea that the gospel needs to be preached to all the nations sounds like something that hasn't happened yet, Colossians 1:23 shows that early Christians took the prediction in terms of the Roman world, not the entire globe.

When Christ calls a man, he bids him come and die.

—DIETRICH BONHOEFFER

EXAMINE

The Jewish War took place in the years leading up to the destruction of the temple. Other "rumors of war" in the A.D. 60s included one that the Parthians were going to attack the Roman Empire from the east. We know of at least two messianic pretenders, one named Theudas and the other known simply as "the Egyptian" (compare Acts 5:36; 21:38). We know of a famine in Acts 11, and that an earthquake destroyed Colossae around A.D. 61. It is not difficult to believe that some Christians lost their lives in the lead-up to Jerusalem's end, although the only life-threatening persecution we know of took place at the hands of Nero around the year A.D. 64.

EXPLORE

Christians will not always face persecution, but we should not be surprised if we do. If we do, we should face it for the right reasons. There is a certain mentality that brings unnecessary persecution on itself and then thinks itself righteous for suffering. And there's no virtue in a self-created persecution. Someone who abrasively confronts others "in the name of truth" may face hostility not because of the truth, but because he or she is tactless. So some Christian activists do God no favors when they cultivate anti-Christian sentiment just because they have a personality that has to win.

PRAYER

Father, teach me to suffer not because I cannot resist fighting, but because I am willing to face the cross and follow you in submission.

Day 3

THE TEMPLE DEFILED
Mark 13:14–23

INTRODUCTION

Jesus now described the moment when the temple would be destroyed. He drew on the apocalyptic language of Daniel to point to a time of unspeakable woe.

ENGAGE

Mark 13 predicted that things would get worse and worse in the lead-up to the temple's destruction. Verse 19 speaks of days of unequaled distress, and verse 20 says no one would have survived if God did not cut those days short. It is understandable that many prophecy teachers have thought these words must surely relate to the end times rather than to the time before the destruction of the temple in A.D. 70. It is of course possible that the two events are blurred together, as seems to take place sometimes with "apocalyptic" imagery. For example, it is interesting that Luke's version of this prophecy takes those two statements out. On the other hand, perhaps we should take that language as hyperbole in the first place.

As we have opportunity, let us do good to all people, especially to those who belong to the family of believers.

—GALATIANS 6:10

EXAMINE

The idea of an "abomination that causes desolation" comes from Daniel 11:31, which originally referred to the desecration of the Jerusalem temple in 167 B.C. by Syrians who lived to the extreme north of Israel. However, Jesus used the image in relation to the impending destruction of the Jerusalem temple in A.D. 70. In fact, Luke 21:20 paraphrases Jesus' prediction to refer explicitly to the surrounding of Jerusalem by armies, which took place in the lead-up to the city's destruction. Tradition holds that the Christians of Jerusalem did flee to a city called Pella during that time, as Mark 13:14

instructed. The need to flee immediately may reflect what happened during a siege—once the city was surrounded, no one would be going in or out.

EXPLORE

It can make a difference if you are convinced that things are going to get worse or better. The historical pessimist may not be motivated to work for long-term change because he or she is convinced things will only get worse. It can even become a self-fulfilling prophecy when a person actually blocks the progress that is possible or does nothing to stop evil when he or she could. It is much better for the person for whom a historical optimism becomes a self-fulfilling prophecy. This person, not knowing whether God intends to allow things to get worse, just might affect the world for the better. It's clear which bias we should tend toward. Let us work for the good in any opportunity we see!

PRAYER

Father, help me to see every possible opportunity to do good in the world. Give me the strength to jump through those open doors with gladness.

Day 4

THE SECOND COMING
Mark 13:24–31

INTRODUCTION

Jesus now moved from the topic of the temple's destruction to Jesus' return from heaven to judge the earth and reign as its king. The two topics blur into one another in Mark 13.

ENGAGE

The sun will darken; the moon will turn to blood; stars will fall from the sky (13:24–25). Mark may not have wanted us to take this imagery literally, even in terms of how things will appear to people looking on. Acts 2:20 uses this same picture to talk about the day of Pentecost, so the meaning could be something like saying, "It will be an earth-shattering event." Then the "Son of Man" will come on the clouds (Mark 13:26), an image that comes from Daniel 7:13. In Daniel, a heavenly figure comes to rule over the entire earth, which Jesus will do when he returns. While some scholars think this is a metaphor for the destruction of Jerusalem, most think Jesus meant this statement literally.

EXAMINE

One of the more puzzling predictions in this passage is, "This generation will certainly not pass away until all these things have happened" (Mark 13:30). Certainly that prediction became true in relation to the destruction of Jerusalem. It just didn't happen in relation to Jesus' return to earth. Other interpretations have been suggested, such as perhaps Jesus meant the generation after Israel became a nation again in 1948, after the fig tree budded (13:28–29). But such a meaning is not at all clear from what Mark actually says. Perhaps the word *generation* should actually be translated *race*, that the human race will not pass away until it happens. In the end, it is just a difficult statement to interpret.

EXPLORE

It is two thousand years later and Jesus' words have not passed away. We are still reading them. We are hopefully still listening to them. Some of them seem fairly easy to understand: "Love your neighbor." It is much, much harder to apply to our own lives. Indeed, sometimes it seems like the most understandable of Jesus' teachings are some of the most difficult to put into action. Still other sayings we resist, such as Jesus' clear ethic on giving away as much of our money as possible. Then there is teaching like this one that is extremely difficult to understand. These passages make us humble and remind us that we will never be able to know everything in this world.

God, grant me the serenity to accept the things
I cannot change, the courage to change the things
I can, and the wisdom to know the difference.

—RICHARD NIEBUHR

PRAYER

Jesus, give me the strength to apply the teaching I understand, the courage to apply the teaching I resist, and the humility to admit when I do not understand.

Day 5

THE DAY AND HOUR
Mark 13:32–37

INTRODUCTION

These well-known verses remind us that while we may be able to sense that Jesus' approach is near, we will never know the precise day or hour. Every single person who has made such a prediction thus far in history has been wrong.

ENGAGE

No one knows the precise time of Jesus' return. In fact, these well-known verses reveal to us that Jesus himself did not know while he was on earth. Although now in heaven he presumably has returned to an "all knowing" state, he did not know all things while he was on earth, including the precise time he would come back to earth. The angels in heaven did not know either. The key is that the house needs to be ready when the master returns. We are the servants of the house. We keep the house ready as if our Lord were to come back any day. In the meantime, we continue about his mission. We continue to share the good news of the kingdom.

EXAMINE

Matthew 25 gives us some additional parables that reinforce the brief teaching in Mark. One is the parable of the ten virgins (Matt. 25:1–13). Five of them kept their lamps and oil ready for the bridegroom's return, but five missed the wedding because they did not stay ready. A second one is the parable of the talents (25:14–30). A master leaves gold with three servants, who are expected to use what he has left them while he is gone. The final one is the parable of the sheep and the goats (25:31–46), where the Son of Man assigns various eternal destinies to individuals at the judgment. The basis for their eternal destination is how they have treated those who are poor and in need.

EXPLORE

Countless prophecy teachers for the last 150 years have ignored the warnings of these verses and tried to set exact dates for when Jesus will return. One of the more striking examples was a little book called *Eighty-Eight Reasons Why the Lord Is Returning in 1988*. It is astounding to realize that every single one of the countless people who have made predictions about Jesus' return in all of history have been completely and embarrassingly wrong. The obvious conclusion is that you shouldn't guess when Jesus will return. You are far more likely to learn about obscure current events from contemporary prophecy teaching than to learn anything about Jesus' return. Jesus will return to earth one day. Be ready and leave it at that.

O land of rest, for thee I sigh! When will the moment come when I shall lay my armor by and dwell in peace at home? We'll work till Jesus comes and we'll be gathered home.

—ELIZABETH MILLS

PRAYER

Jesus, strengthen me for the long haul of history. Help me to never get tired of doing good or get distracted with speculation about the timing of your return.

BRIDGING JESUS' WORLD AND OURS

In the passages for this week, we have seen Jesus' foresight, his ability to see what is coming. Mark 13 especially was a blueprint for the church of the first century to follow in the lead-up to the destruction of the temple. Also blurred into those prophetic words are some words about Jesus' final return to earth, when he will finally set the world straight for good.

How did Jesus know these things? We often have a stereotyped view of prophecy, and it may well be that Jesus had this particular kind of gift of prophecy, when God tells someone something that no one else could possibly predict. But there is a much more useful—and much more common—sense of spiritual foresight that many key Christians have today.

Perhaps you could call it a certain kind of discernment. There are those who see what is coming in the next weeks, months, or even years. They see it well before everyone else. It is a gift that God gives certain people, and there are many within the church who have it. The church should identify these people and rely heavily on them as we move forward.

EXERCISE

Are you someone who buries your "talent" in the ground? Do you trust God enough to risk using the gifts he has given you for the benefit of God's people and others? Examine yourself this week. If you need to risk more for God, resolve to do so, with God's help.

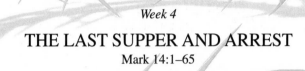

THE LAST SUPPER AND ARREST
Mark 14:1–65

"*Abba*, Father," he said, "everything is possible for you.
Take this cup from me. Yet not what I will, but what you will."

—MARK 14:36

Day 1

JESUS' ANOINTING
Mark 14:1–11

INTRODUCTION

On Tuesday night, just two days before the Passover meal, Jesus dined in Bethany, about two miles from Jerusalem. A woman anointed Jesus while he was eating in the home of Simon the leper.

ENGAGE

Given how great an emphasis Jesus put on taking care of the poor, it is striking in this passage that Jesus said, "The poor you will always have with you" (14:7). Someone standing there had criticized this woman for wasting her perfume to anoint Jesus. He protested that the woman didn't have her priorities straight (in John it was Judas Iscariot who criticized). But Jesus disagreed.

Ultimately, he is more important than any other human being, especially at this moment before his death. This story is a reminder that, ultimately, Jesus is the object of our worship. We can debate whether he wants us to use our resources to build cathedrals in his honor, but he is certainly worthy of them and the whole universe.

EXAMINE

Human nature finds it so easy to hide sinful attitudes behind a veneer of spirituality. In this case, perhaps the critical man was jealous of the attention the woman was giving Jesus. Maybe he was jealous of the attention itself. Maybe he was jealous because it was a person of the opposite sex giving Jesus the attention. Whatever the reason, Jesus called him out on it. There was nothing wrong with the heart of the woman. She was not making some sort of advance toward Jesus. She was not trying to get anyone's praise or attention. She was just honoring her Lord. Meanwhile, the man was showing the ugliness of his heart.

EXPLORE

All four gospels tell this story, although they differ a little on the details. In Matthew, Mark, and Luke, the woman who anointed Jesus is anonymous. But Jesus predicted that the story of this woman would be retold wherever the gospel is preached, and this devotional is proof that her story goes on. This woman, perhaps Mary the sister of Lazarus (John 12:3), is a testimony to how God can use anyone. Are not most of God's servants the nameless Christians of the ages who have faithfully believed and served the Lord? Are not you and I the same as this woman? God does not require that we do big things but that we serve him faithfully with what we have.

Jesus, name above all names, beautiful Savior,
glorious Lord, Emmanuel, God is with us,
Blessed Redeemer, Living Word.

—NAIDA HEARN

PRAYER

Jesus, in all my efforts to do good in your world, help me not to forget that you are more important than any good I might do. I worship you above all.

Day 2

THE LAST SUPPER
Mark 14:12–26

INTRODUCTION

Jesus ate the Passover meal with his disciples after sundown on Thursday night. This meal was the basis for the Communion sacrament that churches have celebrated ever since.

ENGAGE

What we now celebrate as a small part of a service was originally a meal, both on the night Jesus ate his Last Supper and in the early church. The Lord's Supper in the early church was probably a "love feast" something like church potlucks today, although it is possible that at places like Corinth, a wealthy church member might provide food. During the meal, Jesus broke bread and compared it to his body, which was about to be broken. Then after supper, he passed around a cup of wine and compared it to the blood he was about to shed. He predicted that he would not drink wine again until the kingdom of God had arrived.

The principal fruit of receiving the Eucharist in Holy Communion is an intimate union with Christ Jesus.

—ROMAN CATHOLIC CATECHISM, 1391

EXAMINE

Jesus gave instructions to some of his disciples similar to the instructions he gave on Palm Sunday. They were to go into town; they would meet someone; this person would show them a room to use for the Passover meal. Mark is not clear about whether this was an instance of Jesus' knowing the future or if Jesus had prearranged with this person to use the room. The two disciples then made preparations for the meal. What a tone the night must have had! What a heaviness! Judas left to betray Jesus. While they may have expected Jesus to become king in Jerusalem, it was now beginning to sink in that he was going to die.

EXPLORE

Some churches don't take Communion very often. They might be afraid it will lose its meaning if it is done too often. But you could use this argument of almost anything: "Let's not have Sunday service every week so it will be more meaningful when we have it." In the end, it's up to us for Communion to be meaningful anytime it takes place. Many think of Communion as a time to hit the reset button on their faith. It's a time for confession of sin and repentance. But for others, it's a great time to soak up God's grace, period. To them, it is truly a sacrament, a place God has set aside to meet us and energize our faith, hope, and love.

PRAYER

Jesus, help me not to miss what you want to do for me in Communion. Open up my heart to more grace than I could possibly imagine.

Day 3

GETHSEMANE
Mark 14:32–42

INTRODUCTION

Jesus and his disciples prayed in a garden at the
Mount of Olives. It is possible that they were hiding
nearby for the night, but Judas knew where they were
and was in the process of betraying Jesus as he prayed.

ENGAGE

It is deeply encouraging to know that Jesus genuinely
wrestled with the task before him. While we shouldn't
doubt his ultimate resolve to do God's will, he clearly
would have preferred another option. It reminds us that
it is not a sin to be tempted. After all, Jesus was tempted
in every way just as we are but didn't make the *choice* to
sin (compare Heb. 4:15). While we should be optimistic

about the power of God to make it easy to do the right thing, sometimes we will have to push through temptation by the power of the Spirit. God will not let us get into a situation where we cannot do the right thing by his grace (1 Cor. 10:13).

EXAMINE

"The spirit is willing, but the flesh is weak" (Mark 14:38). How many of us resonate with this verse! We may have a strong desire to do the right thing and do good in the world, yet we can be so exhausted that we can barely bring ourselves to do anything. We may have no intention of arguing with our spouse or losing our temper with our children, but it happens because we are tired or in a hurry. John Wesley called these sorts of events "sins of surprise." They are incidents where, because we are not getting enough sleep or not being careful about our commitments, we put our flesh in a situation where we may have a hard time overcoming temptation.

EXPLORE

Jesus implied that prayer can be a strong ally in overcoming temptation. He also implied that we can prepare for temptation. It is true that emotions are not sinful. It is not sinful to get angry. It is not sinful to be despondent. But sin can be involved when we have not been preparing ourselves for the moment of temptation. How we respond to the moment of crisis can reveal what we have been doing in the lead-up to that moment. Have we been so surrendered to God's will that it is not difficult to surrender to him in the time of uncertainty? Have we been communicating so regularly with him that we don't feel his absence in the time of trial?

In some instances, our being surprised [by sin]
is owing to some willful and culpable neglect, or,
to a sleepiness of soul which might have been
prevented, or shaken off before the temptation came.

—JOHN WESLEY

PRAYER

Spirit, give me insights into the ways in which I manage myself and my time. Give me the foresight and providence to avoid the weakness of the flesh.

Day 4

JESUS' ARREST
Mark 14:43–52

INTRODUCTION

Judas had arranged to show Jesus' location to individuals from the chief priests, teachers of the law, and the Jerusalem elders. They found Jesus in the garden of Gethsemane and arrested him.

ENGAGE

It is hard to know what exactly Judas was thinking when he betrayed Jesus. Was he disillusioned with Jesus? Had he come to Jerusalem thinking that Jesus was the Messiah, only to be disappointed? Or did he think he was forcing God's hand? Did he think that Jesus would certainly not allow the mob to arrest him? Matthew records that Judas later became remorseful when he saw that Jesus was in trouble, that he tried to take back his part in Jesus' arrest. But he couldn't (see Matt. 27:3–5). That could indicate that he hadn't expected things to develop as they did. In the end, he would commit suicide and the disciples would replace his spot among the Twelve.

Any coward can fight a battle when he's sure of winning, but give me the man who has pluck to fight when he's sure of losing.

—George Eliot

EXAMINE

One disciple standing with Jesus drew his sword and cut off someone's ear (John tells us Peter did it). But then when Jesus acquiesced to the mob and prepared to go with them, the disciples scattered and deserted Jesus. This is where we find the peculiar story of an anonymous young man who lost his garment in the confusion and ran away naked (Mark 14:51–52). (Many scholars speculate that the young man might actually have been the author of Mark.) Is it possible that the followers of Jesus were prepared to fight against any enemy but were not prepared for Jesus to just go silently with his opponents? Is it possible that, far from being cowards, they were just very, very confused?

EXPLORE

There is a certain kind of Christian who is more than ready to fight for Jesus. Some Christians seem to relish getting involved in politics and trying to get candidates elected they believe will advance a Christian agenda. Maybe someone will work to get a particular law passed or defeated in the name of Christ. They may be more than willing to fight with Christ to win over the Devil. But are they also able to lose with Christ? If it is God's will to allow some other candidate or party to win, if it is God's will to allow the other side to prevail, will they flee then? What if it is God's will for you at this time to suffer rather than win?

PRAYER

Jesus, make me willing not only to join you in the fight against the Devil, but to lose battles, knowing that you have already won the war.

Day 5

THE SANHEDRIN
Mark 14:53–65

INTRODUCTION

In Mark, Jesus appeared more or less before the entire Sanhedrin, the Jewish ruling council. After a number of false witnesses testified, the high priest finally got the confession he was looking for.

ENGAGE

After Jesus' "trial" went on for some time, Jesus finally confessed that he in fact was the Messiah, the Son of God. He confessed that he was the Son of Man figure from Daniel 7, who would come on the clouds of heaven to rule the nations of the earth. This open statement of Jesus' identity was all the more remarkable given that Jesus had generally hidden his identity throughout the gospel of Mark. He had silenced the demons and instructed those he healed not to talk about him. Before, it would have been counterproductive to acknowledge his identity. They would have tried to make him king then and there. But now it was no problem to confess openly that he was—and is—Israel's promised king.

EXAMINE

The high priest and leaders of Jerusalem seem to have had a whole group of false witnesses ready to testify against Jesus. They were armed with half-truths. They accused Jesus of saying treacherous things against the temple when in fact what Jesus had been critiquing was them and their administration of Israel. It was not the temple so much that needed to be destroyed, but they needed to be removed as Israel's leaders. They took literally things that Jesus meant figuratively. When others are out to get us, they are looking for any open door. We may not get a chance to defend ourselves, and Jesus ultimately showed us how to suffer injustice when it was God's will to allow it to prevail.

EXPLORE

It never seemed to enter the high priest's mind that Jesus might actually *be* the Messiah. He had his mind made up, and he was only looking to reinforce it. What a human tendency! We are so convinced God is on our side that we hardly even stop to consider the possibility that we may actually be wrong or misguided. Like the high priest, we are just waiting to rip our clothes in feigned distress over something. But it is all a show. In such cases, we aren't really interested in the truth or in what is right *to God*. We are really only feeding our own egos and are angry that someone dares to oppose us and our positions.

PRAYER

Father, help me never assume that my position must surely be the right position, but in my submission to you, help me bend my mind to *your* truth.

Lord, where we are wrong, make us willing to change; where we are right, make us easy to live with.

—PETER MARSHALL

BRIDGING JESUS' WORLD AND OURS

In the passages for this week, we see Jesus' temptation, and we see emotions like sorrow and discouragement, as well as his resolve. Jesus prayed in the garden of

Gethsemane for God to let the suffering ahead pass if at all possible. He was surely tempted to run away. It would have been so easy. He was already outside the city walls. He only needed to walk two miles to Bethany.

He was discouraged when his core disciples couldn't even stay awake with him. But he didn't show any hesitation once the final sequence of events was in motion. He showed no hesitation at his arrest or in his appearance before the Jewish leaders.

May we follow Jesus' example when we face trials and persecution. We should not be hard on ourselves when we dread its approach, when we want to be rescued from facing it. We should not be worried that we are tempted to run the other way. But may we take the next step when it comes. One step after the next, we endure. The thought of the whole trial may be daunting, but God will see us through each next step.

EXERCISE

Are you currently facing a major trial or period of suffering? If you have felt guilty for doubt or sorrow, let go of that guilt by God's grace. But if you need to step forward, take that next step in faith, knowing that God will see you through.

Week 5

BETRAYAL AND CRUCIFIXION
Mark 14:27–31; 14:66—15:47

The curtain of the temple was torn in two from
top to bottom. And when the centurion, who stood
there in front of Jesus, saw how he died, he said,
"Surely this man was the Son of God!"

—MARK 15:38–39

Day 1

PETER'S DENIAL
Mark 14:27–31, 66–72

INTRODUCTION

At the Last Supper, Jesus had predicted that Peter would deny him three times. While Jesus was being interrogated by the Jewish leaders and high priest, Peter was nearby, denying any knowledge of Jesus.

ENGAGE

Peter was so emphatic that he would never deny Jesus, but that was several hours ago when he was still ready to fight to the death. That was before Jesus submitted to those who had come to arrest him and went willingly. That was before Peter began to seriously question whether Jesus was really the Messiah. And when the rooster crowed, it all came home that he had done exactly what

Jesus predicted he would do. Imagine the guilt he would later carry, knowing that his doubts were misplaced and that he had failed his Lord and friend. It is an encouragement to us to get back up when we fail. God can still go on to use us in spectacular ways.

EXAMINE

Perhaps for most of us, our typical reaction when we are caught doing wrong is denial: Criminals do it; it happens in marriage; it happens in the classroom; it happens in the church. Someone does something they know is wrong: cheat on a test, cheat on a spouse, steal money from the church or work place, get caught in a lie. The first reaction is almost always denial. In Peter's case, he was not doing anything wrong, but he was in a dangerous place, and his faith was wavering inside. His faith was not strong enough to survive these circumstances. He failed his Lord. We won't finish a race if we haven't been training, and Peter's faith was flabby.

EXPLORE

Sometimes it is hard to know exactly what we will do until the actual time of crisis. Christians always need to be in faith training. We often can't anticipate when the next trial is going to come or exactly what that trial is going to be. That calls for a spiritual "fitness" regimen that keeps us strong all around. It means regular prayer, because we'll need a good communication system in place for the time of battle. We'll need to know how to call for backup. It means regular meditation on God's Word and the rich growth the Spirit brings through it. It means the support network of other believers, which we get through regular fellowship and worship together.

Run in such a way as to get the prize. Everyone who
competes in the games goes into strict training. . . .
Therefore I do not run like someone running
aimlessly; I do not fight like a boxer beating the
air. No, I strike a blow to my body and make it my
slave so that after I have preached to others,
I myself will not be disqualified for the prize.

—1 CORINTHIANS 9:24–27

PRAYER

Spirit, coach me continually to become spiritually fit. Remind me to avail myself regularly of the means of grace God has given me.

Day 2

PILATE
Mark 15:1–15

INTRODUCTION

The Jewish leaders brought Jesus to Pilate since only Pilate was officially allowed to put someone to death. Perhaps they knew he was already going to crucify some criminals that day and hoped to include Jesus among them.

ENGAGE

Jesus knew what was happening on a bigger scale than anyone else around him. He was about to die as a ransom for the sins of all humanity. There was no need to talk. It was not God's will to stop what was happening. Meeting with Pilate was a mere formality in the process of dying for the sins of the world. For most of us, meeting with someone like Pilate would be a major event full of terror.

Surely Pilate thought it would be a major event for this man from Galilee—he was used to being a big deal. But for Jesus, Pilate was nothing, an insignificant cog in the wheel of a redemption plan that started before the foundations of the world.

EXAMINE

To Pilate, this encounter was scarcely important, nor was putting someone to death a big deal for him. He probably didn't even interview most criminals before consigning them to the cross. But Jesus had committed no crime. He had just gotten under the skin of the Jerusalem leaders. In itself that fact might have predisposed Pilate to show mercy on him, to annoy the power brokers of Israel. Jesus didn't beg for his life, something Pilate must have found intriguing. Looking from the outside, Pilate must have found the notion that this person was in competition with Caesar ridiculous. He probably was more than willing to dismiss Jesus as a crazy. However, Matthew tells us that Pilate's wife was warned about Jesus in a dream (Matt. 27:19).

EXPLORE

Given our humanity, it is hard not to treat things like death or hardship as major events. Hopefully we know that God is all in all and that we are the smallest speck in a massive universe. Hopefully we know that any hardships we experience are "light and momentary troubles" (2 Cor. 4:17). Hopefully we know that death is but a short pause in an eternity of life. But it's hard for that knowledge to make it through to our nerves and emotions. Jesus gave us the model. He seemed to hardly notice that Pilate was in the room. Jesus was perhaps the most silent of all the people involved in his arrest and trial.

By faith [Moses] left Egypt, not fearing the king's anger;
he persevered because he saw him who is invisible.

—HEBREWS 11:27

PRAYER

Spirit, help the true priorities of life and death sink in and permeate the whole of my being so that I can stand easily in the day of trial.

Day 3

THE CRUCIFIXION
Mark 15:16–32

INTRODUCTION

The Roman soldiers mocked Jesus as they got him ready for crucifixion, putting a purple robe on him and a crown of thorns on his head. Then at nine in the morning, they crucified him. The mocking continued.

ENGAGE

The obscure names in the passion story remind us that this story is real. There were real people named Simon, Alexander, and Rufus who suddenly found themselves part of a story that would last forever, a story that God had planned since forever. Simon carried the cross for Jesus as he was passing by. It must have had an immense effect on him. The fact that the names of him and his children were known to Mark implies that he and his children became believers as a result. This is an amazing thing to ponder. After carrying Jesus' cross, rather than become convinced that Jesus was a fake, they started a journey that ended with them becoming his followers.

Well might the sun in darkness hide, and shut his glories in, when Christ, the mighty Maker died, for man the creature's sin.

—ISAAC WATTS

EXAMINE

To the Roman soldiers, Jesus was just a crazy Jew who bizarrely thought he could challenge the Roman Empire. They put a robe on him meant to mimic a king's robe. They twisted some thorns together and made a fake crown, humiliating Jesus. They acted like they were bowing down to him. Then they got violent. They spit on him and struck him on the head. But as Isaiah 53:7 puts it, "As a sheep before its shearers is silent, so he did not open his mouth." As with Pilate, Jesus was simply playing out his destiny as Savior of the world. Ironically, he was dying so that the very people who were beating him might have the chance to be saved.

EXPLORE

It is so hard to watch the wicked prevail. We have this sense of justice that says the good guy has to win. The bad guy has to be found out and punished. By faith we believe that God will bring this sort of justice about in the end. But it doesn't always happen in this life and even when it does happen in this life, it can take years. Sometimes we helplessly stand by as someone does wrong or we experience wrong. What strength it takes to keep our mouths shut when we know speaking won't change anything! What power it takes to endure when we know it is God's will!

PRAYER

Jesus, help me not to take the momentary power of the wicked too seriously. Help me to see that you are still in control, no matter how hopeless things look.

Day 4

THE END OF DEATH
Mark 15:33–41

INTRODUCTION

At about noon, the whole sky became overcast. Then, at about three in the afternoon, Jesus finally died. He was on the cross for six hours before he cried out his last. Then the curtain of the temple ripped from top to bottom.

ENGAGE

The climax of Mark, the highest point of emotion in the whole story, is when the centurion standing at the cross saw how Jesus died and exclaimed, "Surely this man was the Son of God" (15:39). We don't know if he had been one of the ones mocking Jesus earlier, but he was the only one in all of Mark who saw the connection between Jesus' death and his identity as Messiah. Peter and others understood that Jesus was the Messiah, but they saw Jesus' suffering as a contradiction to that claim. It was thus not even a Jew who got it first. This centurion was a type of all the non-Jews who would come to believe in Jesus in the centuries to come.

EXAMINE

Although Mark didn't make any comment on what it meant, the ripping of the temple curtain from top to bottom surely symbolized the truth that the book of Hebrews later put so well. The veil that prevented direct access of everyone to God was removed with Jesus' sacrificial death. We can now "approach God's throne of grace with confidence, so that we may receive mercy and find grace to help us in our time of need" (Heb. 4:16). We might also think of Ephesians 2:14, which talks about how Christ "has destroyed the barrier, the dividing wall of hostility" that used to divide Jew and Gentile. We are now a priesthood of believers, and we all have direct access to God's throne.

EXPLORE

Christians have never settled on just one significance for Christ's death. Rather, there are several truths we can see in it. For example, it was the defeat of death

(Heb. 2:14) so that we might live forever. Christ died "for our sins" (1 Cor. 15:3) as the Passover Lamb (1 Cor. 5:7). The ancients sometimes thought of sacrifices as satisfying the anger of God, and Christians today sometimes think of it satisfying the justice of God (compare Rom. 3:25–26). Another way to say it is that it satisfies the order of things. Mark 10:45 likens Jesus' death to a "ransom" for sins. Romans 5:8 talks about what a tremendous demonstration of love it was. All these pictures are true.

Therefore, brothers and sisters, since we have confidence to enter the Most Holy Place by the blood of Jesus, by a new and living way opened for us through the curtain, that is, his body, and since we have a great priest over the house of God, let us draw near to God with a sincere heart and with the full assurance that faith brings.

—HEBREWS 10:19–22

PRAYER

Jesus, thank you for your humble obedience to the point of death. May I be willing to do no less than give my all for you.

Day 5

JESUS' BURIAL
Mark 15:42–47

INTRODUCTION

Because the Sabbath was approaching at dusk, they quickly placed Jesus' body in a tomb in the rock, with a stone rolled against its entrance. The women took note of where he was buried so they could return on Sunday to anoint his body.

ENGAGE

In these verses, we meet Joseph of Arimathea for the first time. The specific names remind us again of how real this story is. These people would not have been remembered so specifically if they had not remained known to the Christian community long after the resurrection. Joseph of Arimathea was on the Jewish Sanhedrin, apparently a significant person politically in Jerusalem. He was important enough to have access to Pilate. He bought some linen and wrapped Jesus' body in it. Then he put Jesus in his personal tomb, one cut into the rock with a circular stone at its entrance. Mary Magdalene and other women who had supported Jesus' needs during his ministry had been following at a distance.

When the perishable has been clothed with the imperishable, and the mortal with immortality, then the saying that is written will come true: "Death has been swallowed up in victory." "Where, O death, is your victory? Where, O death, is your sting?"

—1 CORINTHIANS 15:54–55

EXAMINE

Pilate was amazed at how quickly Jesus died. In John's gospel, they actually broke the legs of those hanging with him so that they would die more quickly. Sometimes you hear people wonder if Jesus died from the stress of God's abandonment. He cried out, "My God, my God, why have you forsaken me?" (Mark 15:34). Jesus was of course quoting Scripture (Ps. 22:1). There is no theological or biblical evidence that God turned his face away from Jesus because Jesus was taking on our sins. That sort of thinking comes from centuries after the Bible. However, the fact that God had not really abandoned him does not minimize the injustice of the moment or the abandonment Jesus may have felt at that moment.

EXPLORE

The day that Jesus died was the darkest day of all history. Some versions of the Apostle's Creed at this point say, "He descended into hell." For some Christians, it seemed important for Jesus actually to dip into hell so that he could fully experience the punishment that we deserve. But there is no biblical evidence for this theology. A better version of the creed translates the phrase as, "He descended to the dead." First Peter gives us hints that Jesus visited the other dead, perhaps both to confirm the destiny of the wicked and to announce the good news of resurrection to the righteous. Now when we die, we immediately enter the presence of the Lord, although still awaiting the coming resurrection.

PRAYER

Thank you, Jesus, for enduring the cross, for despising the shame, for tasting death for everyone. Thank you for sanctifying death so that I might not fear it.

BRIDGING JESUS' WORLD AND OURS

In the passages for this week, we see the heart of Jesus' suffering. Christians believe that only Jesus could do what he did on Good Friday. Only Jesus as God come to earth could die for the sins of the world. Only the death of this sinless human could be a sufficient sacrifice to bring the universe back into order.

Our job is to trust in him. Our job is to be buried in baptism with him so that we die to our old self, the person that used to be a slave to sin. We cannot die to sin in our own power. It is in fact God's power that joins us to Christ.

We may fail him, although we do not have to. Peter and Judas both failed Jesus after following him for three years. We do not have to fail him, for he is looking for our hearts, not our perfection. But if we do fail him, Peter and Judas are two types of failure. The first found a place of repentance, and God rejoices at his return. The second hardened his heart beyond repair.

EXERCISE

Have you failed God recently? If so, are you on a Peter or Judas trajectory? The Judas trajectory can't bring itself to truly repent. But the Peter trajectory gets back up and continues on the right course. Resolve to get back up and move forward again with God's help.

Week 6

RESURRECTION
Mark 16:1–8

You are looking for Jesus the Nazarene, who was crucified. He has risen! He is not here. See the place where they laid him. But go, tell his disciples and Peter, "He is going ahead of you into Galilee. There you will see him, just as he told you."

—MARK 16:6–7

Day 1

THE WITNESS OF THE WOMEN
Mark 16:1–3

INTRODUCTION

The first witnesses to the empty tomb were Mary Magdalene and other women who came to the tomb to anoint Jesus' body. According to John 20, Mary was also the first one to whom Jesus appeared after he rose from the dead.

ENGAGE

Jesus was buried on Friday so quickly and under such difficult circumstances that the normal preparations for burial were not possible. The Sabbath was approaching at sundown, and they hastily put Jesus in a tomb meant for someone named Joseph of Arimathea. Mary Magdalene and another Mary took note of where Jesus was buried

(Mark 15:47). Mary Magdalene had followed Jesus for some time after Jesus cast demons out of her (Luke 8:2). She and some other women apparently supported Jesus and his disciples from their own resources (Luke 8:3). Some of these women came early Sunday morning to finish the normal burial process. They went without knowing how they would manage to move the heavy stone in place to seal off the tomb.

EXAMINE

Perhaps nowhere do the differences between the Gospels stand out more than when we compare the different resurrection accounts. But from a historical standpoint, I do not believe we should find this observation discouraging. In the differing gospel accounts, we can see the tsunami waves of an astounding event that rushed across time and space in the first century. It started with an empty tomb first discovered by women. Surely no one in the ancient world would make up this part of the story. The culture in general didn't consider women to be particularly credible. So the historical likelihood that we are hearing what happened at this point seems strong. The empty tomb was discovered Sunday morning by women going to anoint Jesus' body.

EXPLORE

Hopefully all Christians today agree that women and men are of equal value and significance in God's eyes, even when we debate over what roles God prefers them to play. We must also address the prominent roles they sometimes played in the Bible. At times they were supreme political (Judg. 4:4–8) and religious (2 Kings 22:14) leaders. They were prophets (Acts 2:17–18), deacons (Rom. 16:1), and apostles (Rom. 16:7). They discipled ministers (Acts 18:26). In John, Jesus even chose to appear first to Mary Magdalene, not to Peter or any of the other disciples (John 20:10–18). If God calls you do to something, you must do it, whether you are a woman or a man.

There is neither Jew nor Gentile, neither slave nor free, nor is there male and female, for you are all one in Christ Jesus.

—GALATIANS 3:28

PRAYER

Father, help me not to create artificial boundaries in relation to what any person can or cannot do. Help me submit to whomever you call to do whatever you command.

Day 2

THE EMPTY TOMB
Mark 16:4–5

INTRODUCTION

When the women finally arrived, they found the large stone in front of the tomb moved and the tomb itself empty. Instead, a young man in a white robe was there.

ENGAGE

The empty tomb is a key element in any historical argument for Jesus' resurrection. The surprise of the women is overwhelmingly clear in Mark 16:8. In fact, despite some diversity among the resurrection accounts, they all unanimously point to immense surprise and confusion by Jesus' followers when no one could find his body. They simply weren't expecting it. They would certainly have exhausted every possible avenue to find his body once they realized it was missing. Then Jesus' resurrection appearances finish off the argument. Paul told us about numerous people who saw Jesus alive, giving tradition in 1 Corinthians 15 that is actually earlier than any of the gospel accounts by some twenty years. A lot of people were absolutely convinced Jesus appeared to them.

God sent his Son, they called him Jesus; he came to love,
heal, and forgive. He lived and died to buy my pardon;
an empty grave is there to prove my Savior lives!

—BILL GAITHER

EXAMINE

Matthew's gospel tells us about an event that the other Gospels do not, namely, the posting of a guard at the tomb. After Jesus died, some chief priests and Pharisees went to Pilate to warn him about the possibility that the disciples might try to steal the body (Matt. 27:62–64). Pilate thus allowed the Jewish leaders to post a guard at Jesus' tomb. When the angel of the Lord appeared, they shook and became like corpses (28:4). Then the chief priests bribed the guards to say that the disciples had stolen the body, a rumor that existed over forty years later when Matthew was probably written. This fact shows that even those who didn't believe in the resurrection admitted that Jesus' body was never found.

EXPLORE

The empty tomb tells us that there was continuity between Jesus' physical body before he died and his resurrection body after he rose again. Some Christians today assume that we lose our bodies forever when we die. They assume that when we die, our spirits go to heaven and that is the end of it. I have even heard of Christians who don't think it matters whether someone ever finds Jesus' body for this reason. At the very least, that isn't how the Gospels or Paul thought of it. For Jesus to be raised was for his physical body to be transformed into something different. So God will start our resurrection body with whatever is left of our mortal body.

PRAYER

Father, give me faith to believe when you do the impossible. When I see the empty tomb, strengthen my heart to believe what I see.

Day 3

HE IS RISEN!
Mark 16:6

INTRODUCTION

The angel at the tomb triumphantly proclaimed that Jesus had risen from the dead, and he showed the women the space where Jesus' body had been laid to prove it.

ENGAGE

Paul told us that Jesus "was raised to life for our justification" (Rom. 4:25), our newfound innocence in God's court. The resurrection also implies spiritual strength to live above the power of sin (for example, Rom. 6:5–7). "If the Spirit of him who raised Jesus from the dead is living in you, he who raised Christ from the dead will also give life to your mortal bodies" (Rom. 8:11). In this part of Romans, Paul was talking about

God's desire to empower us by the Spirit to live above the power of sin, to "give life to [our] mortal bodies." Of course the resurrection was also God's vindication of Jesus and his message while he was on earth.

EXAMINE

The empty tomb is one side of the resurrection equation. The other is the appearances of Jesus to various individuals. Paul gave the earliest list in 1 Corinthians 15:5–8. Jesus appeared to Peter after his death. Next came the others who remained among the twelve disciples, with Judas now gone. All of these received God's command to go and be witnesses to Jesus' resurrection. Paul next mentioned that over five hundred people saw Jesus at one point—very significant indeed! What followed was a second tier of witnesses. First there was James, the brother of Jesus and a number of lesser apostles. Finally, Paul himself was the last to whom Jesus appeared personally, and thus the last apostle.

EXPLORE

Paul more than anyone else in the New Testament boldly told us that because Jesus rose from the dead, we will too someday. One day Jesus "will transform our lowly bodies so that they will be like his glorious body" (Phil. 3:21). "Just as we have borne the image of the earthly man, so shall we bear the image of the heavenly man" (1 Cor. 15:49). "The one who raised the Lord Jesus from the dead will also raise us with Jesus" (2 Cor. 4:14). We are not like those who have no hope. "We will not all sleep, but we will be changed—in a flash, in the twinkling of an eye, at the last trumpet" (1 Cor. 15:51–52).

We were therefore buried with him through baptism into death in order that, just as Christ was raised from the dead through the glory of the Father, we too may live a new life.

—ROMANS 6:4

PRAYER

Jesus, thank you for dying for me so that I can be raised with you one day. Raise me to new spiritual life even now, in this life.

Day 4

GO TO GALILEE!
Mark 16:7

INTRODUCTION

The young man told the women that Jesus would appear to the disciples in Galilee. If Mark originally continued beyond 16:8, we can presume that the story went on to tell about this appearance, as in Matthew.

ENGAGE

Since Matthew was probably "built" out of the gospel of Mark, it is at least possible that Matthew 28 could give us a glimpse of how the original version of Mark ended. In its closing verses, Matthew gives us the Great Commission, where Jesus appeared to the disciples on a mountain in Galilee and told them to make disciples of all nations. Jesus passed his authority on to them, now that he was the cosmic King and promised that he would be with them wherever they went, even to the ends of the earth. He assumed that they would go. The process of making disciples involved the washing of baptism and teaching Jesus' instructions on how to live in this world.

EXAMINE

If Matthew 28 gives us one of Jesus' appearances in Galilee, John 21 gives us the other. Peter and some of the disciples were fishing by the Sea of Galilee. They were having no success, but Jesus told them from the shore to try the right side of the boat. When they did it, they caught a large number of fish. The Beloved Apostle, the source behind the gospel of John, realized that it was Jesus. Then Peter launched into the water toward the shore. The impression we get is that the disciples spent at least a little time in Galilee before returning to Jerusalem to finish out the forty days of Acts 1 before Jesus ascended to heaven.

EXPLORE

The Gospels aren't entirely clear about how Jesus' appearances in Jerusalem fit with his appearances in Galilee, but Mark leads us to think that some of Jesus' earliest appearances were in Galilee. We can picture the disciples rushing back to Jerusalem thereafter to wait for Jesus' return. Luke and Acts don't tell us about the trip to Galilee, about a three-day journey to the north. Meanwhile, Acts 1:6 shows us the disciples expecting Jesus to set up his earthly kingdom right then. Instead, there were at least two thousand more years to go. Like with the disciples, there is still good work for us to do and good news to spread. God doesn't want us to wait around. Let's get to it!

The Church exists for nothing else but to draw men into Christ, to make them little Christs.

—C. S. LEWIS

PRAYER

Jesus, I resolve to work spreading the good news and doing good deeds in your name even as I am waiting for you to return from heaven and set everything straight.

Day 5

FIRST REACTION
Mark 16:8

INTRODUCTION

Mark as we have it ends somewhat surprisingly with the women telling no one because they were afraid. The other Gospels tell us that they went on to overcome their fears and shared their news.

ENGAGE

Matthew 28:17 shockingly says that some followers of Jesus doubted even after he appeared to them in Galilee. In John we hear of the doubts of Thomas in Jerusalem, but his doubts were settled when Jesus appeared a second time to the disciples. This knowledge can be a great encouragement to us when we face doubts, and many of us will at some point. After Thomas overcame his doubts, Jesus commended those who believe even though they have not seen (John 20:29). Jesus also opened the eyes of two followers on their way to a village called Emmaus in Luke 24. They did not see the Scriptures with the eyes of the Spirit, and Jesus opened them.

EXAMINE

We do not have the original copy of Mark. The most intact copies we have come from centuries later. This fact should not trouble anyone, but there are some instances where ancient copies of Mark say something different from other copies. The oldest and most reliable witnesses to how Mark ended stop with verse 8, which is very surprising. The book as we have it ends with the women telling no one. It is quite possible that the original ending was lost at a very early date. The ending you sometimes find here is a mixture of material from the other Gospels. What is most important is to recognize that Mark fully teaches the resurrection and implies Jesus' appearance to his disciples in Galilee.

EXPLORE

How will you respond to the fact that Jesus is risen from the dead? As we now have it, Mark ends with the women being afraid to tell. The other Gospels tell us that they soon overcame their fears and shared with the disciples the good news of the empty tomb and the angelic announcement. Thomas also had his doubts, but God helped him to overcome them. Where are you in your response to the good news of Jesus' resurrection? Do you have doubts? Pray for faith. Do you believe but are afraid of what others will think that you believe in such an amazing miracle? Pray for the confidence to testify to the impossible!

PRAYER

I believe, Lord. Help any unbelief. Conquer any fear. Make me also a confident witness to your victory over death that others may join me in eternal life!

In faith there is enough light for those who want to believe and enough shadows to blind those who don't.

—BLAISE PASCAL

BRIDGING JESUS' WORLD AND OURS

In the passages for this week, we see Jesus' greatest victory, his victory over death. Part of Jesus' resurrection is unique. Jesus uniquely rose from the dead to be enthroned as the cosmic King. "He is Lord; he is Lord. He is risen from the dead and he is Lord," goes the chorus. Its theology is exactly that of passages like Philippians 2:6–11.

But Jesus' resurrection also makes it possible for us to be sons and daughters of God. As Jesus rose from the dead, so God will also raise us to new life, even now. Just as we are buried with Christ in baptism, we rise to new life in this world, to victory over temptation. But God will also raise our mortal bodies one day, at the resurrection.

God also calls us, as he called the men and women before us, to be witnesses to his resurrection. He calls us to be witnesses to the good news that Jesus is Lord and king over all. He calls us to join him on his mission to rescue the perishing and care for the dying.

EXERCISE

Are you a witness to Jesus' lordship? Are you willing for others to know that you are a child and servant of the King? Does your life inspire others to become Jesus' followers as well? Resolve to live a life of witness more than ever before, with God's help.